BLOO1

PRESSURE

TRACKER

· · · · · · · · · · · · · · · · · · · ·

Blood Pressure *Tracker*

DATE	TIME	PRESSURE	PULSE	NOTES

Blood Pressure *Tracker*

DATE	TIME	PRESSURE	PULSE	NOTES

Blood Pressure *Tracker*

DATE	TIME	PRESSURE	PULSE	NOTES

Blood Pressure *Tracker*

DATE	TIME	PRESSURE	PULSE	NOTES

Blood Pressure *Tracker*

DATE	TIME	PRESSURE	PULSE	NOTES

Blood Pressure *Tracker*

DATE	TIME	PRESSURE	PULSE	NOTES

Blood Pressure *Tracker*

DATE	TIME	PRESSURE	PULSE	NOTES

Blood Pressure *Tracker*

DATE	TIME	PRESSURE	PULSE	NOTES

Blood Pressure *Tracker*

DATE	TIME	PRESSURE	PULSE	NOTES

Blood Pressure *Tracker*

DATE	TIME	PRESSURE	PULSE	NOTES

Blood Pressure *Tracker*

DATE	TIME	PRESSURE	PULSE	NOTES

Blood Pressure *Tracker*

DATE	TIME	PRESSURE	PULSE	NOTES

Blood Pressure *Tracker*

DATE	TIME	PRESSURE	PULSE	NOTES

Blood Pressure *Tracker*

DATE	TIME	PRESSURE	PULSE	NOTES

Blood Pressure *Tracker*

DATE	TIME	PRESSURE	PULSE	NOTES

Blood Pressure *Tracker*

DATE	TIME	PRESSURE	PULSE	NOTES

Blood Pressure *Tracker*

DATE	TIME	PRESSURE	PULSE	NOTES

Blood Pressure *Tracker*

DATE	TIME	PRESSURE	PULSE	NOTES

Blood Pressure *Tracker*

DATE	TIME	PRESSURE	PULSE	NOTES

Blood Pressure *Tracker*

DATE	TIME	PRESSURE	PULSE	NOTES

Blood Pressure *Tracker*

DATE	TIME	PRESSURE	PULSE	NOTES

Blood Pressure *Tracker*

DATE	TIME	PRESSURE	PULSE	NOTES

Blood Pressure *Tracker*

DATE	TIME	PRESSURE	PULSE	NOTES

Blood Pressure *Tracker*

DATE	TIME	PRESSURE	PULSE	NOTES

Blood Pressure *Tracker*

DATE	TIME	PRESSURE	PULSE	NOTES

Blood Pressure *Tracker*

DATE	TIME	PRESSURE	PULSE	NOTES

Blood Pressure *Tracker*

DATE	TIME	PRESSURE	PULSE	NOTES

Blood Pressure *Tracker*

DATE	TIME	PRESSURE	PULSE	NOTES

Blood Pressure *Tracker*

DATE	TIME	PRESSURE	PULSE	NOTES

Blood Pressure *Tracker*

DATE	TIME	PRESSURE	PULSE	NOTES

Blood Pressure *Tracker*

DATE	TIME	PRESSURE	PULSE	NOTES

Blood Pressure *Tracker*

DATE	TIME	PRESSURE	PULSE	NOTES

Blood Pressure *Tracker*

DATE	TIME	PRESSURE	PULSE	NOTES

Blood Pressure *Tracker*

DATE	TIME	PRESSURE	PULSE	NOTES

Blood Pressure *Tracker*

DATE	TIME	PRESSURE	PULSE	NOTES

Blood Pressure *Tracker*

DATE	TIME	PRESSURE	PULSE	NOTES

Blood Pressure *Tracker*

DATE	TIME	PRESSURE	PULSE	NOTES

Blood Pressure *Tracker*

DATE	TIME	PRESSURE	PULSE	NOTES

Blood Pressure *Tracker*

DATE	TIME	PRESSURE	PULSE	NOTES

Blood Pressure *Tracker*

DATE	TIME	PRESSURE	PULSE	NOTES

Blood Pressure *Tracker*

DATE	TIME	PRESSURE	PULSE	NOTES

Blood Pressure *Tracker*

DATE	TIME	PRESSURE	PULSE	NOTES

Blood Pressure *Tracker*

DATE	TIME	PRESSURE	PULSE	NOTES

Blood Pressure *Tracker*

DATE	TIME	PRESSURE	PULSE	NOTES

Blood Pressure *Tracker*

DATE	TIME	PRESSURE	PULSE	NOTES

Blood Pressure *Tracker*

DATE	TIME	PRESSURE	PULSE	NOTES

Blood Pressure *Tracker*

DATE	TIME	PRESSURE	PULSE	NOTES

Blood Pressure *Tracker*

DATE	TIME	PRESSURE	PULSE	NOTES

Blood Pressure *Tracker*

DATE	TIME	PRESSURE	PULSE	NOTES

Blood Pressure *Tracker*

DATE	TIME	PRESSURE	PULSE	NOTES

Blood Pressure *Tracker*

DATE	TIME	PRESSURE	PULSE	NOTES

Blood Pressure *Tracker*

DATE	TIME	PRESSURE	PULSE	NOTES

Blood Pressure *Tracker*

DATE	TIME	PRESSURE	PULSE	NOTES

Blood Pressure *Tracker*

DATE	TIME	PRESSURE	PULSE	NOTES

Blood Pressure *Tracker*

DATE	TIME	PRESSURE	PULSE	NOTES

Blood Pressure *Tracker*

DATE	TIME	PRESSURE	PULSE	NOTES

Blood Pressure *Tracker*

DATE	TIME	PRESSURE	PULSE	NOTES

Blood Pressure *Tracker*

DATE	TIME	PRESSURE	PULSE	NOTES

Blood Pressure *Tracker*

DATE	TIME	PRESSURE	PULSE	NOTES

Blood Pressure *Tracker*

DATE	TIME	PRESSURE	PULSE	NOTES

Blood Pressure *Tracker*

DATE	TIME	PRESSURE	PULSE	NOTES

Blood Pressure *Tracker*

DATE	TIME	PRESSURE	PULSE	NOTES

Blood Pressure *Tracker*

DATE	TIME	PRESSURE	PULSE	NOTES

Blood Pressure *Tracker*

DATE	TIME	PRESSURE	PULSE	NOTES

Blood Pressure *Tracker*

DATE	TIME	PRESSURE	PULSE	NOTES

Blood Pressure *Tracker*

DATE	TIME	PRESSURE	PULSE	NOTES

Blood Pressure *Tracker*

DATE	TIME	PRESSURE	PULSE	NOTES

Blood Pressure *Tracker*

DATE	TIME	PRESSURE	PULSE	NOTES

Blood Pressure *Tracker*

DATE	TIME	PRESSURE	PULSE	NOTES

Blood Pressure *Tracker*

DATE	TIME	PRESSURE	PULSE	NOTES

Blood Pressure *Tracker*

DATE	TIME	PRESSURE	PULSE	NOTES

Blood Pressure *Tracker*

DATE	TIME	PRESSURE	PULSE	NOTES

Blood Pressure *Tracker*

DATE	TIME	PRESSURE	PULSE	NOTES

Blood Pressure *Tracker*

DATE	TIME	PRESSURE	PULSE	NOTES

Blood Pressure *Tracker*

DATE	TIME	PRESSURE	PULSE	NOTES

Blood Pressure *Tracker*

DATE	TIME	PRESSURE	PULSE	NOTES

Blood Pressure *Tracker*

DATE	TIME	PRESSURE	PULSE	NOTES

Blood Pressure *Tracker*

DATE	TIME	PRESSURE	PULSE	NOTES

Blood Pressure *Tracker*

DATE	TIME	PRESSURE	PULSE	NOTES

Blood Pressure *Tracker*

DATE	TIME	PRESSURE	PULSE	NOTES

Blood Pressure *Tracker*

DATE	TIME	PRESSURE	PULSE	NOTES

Blood Pressure *Tracker*

DATE	TIME	PRESSURE	PULSE	NOTES

Blood Pressure *Tracker*

DATE	TIME	PRESSURE	PULSE	NOTES

Blood Pressure *Tracker*

DATE	TIME	PRESSURE	PULSE	NOTES

Blood Pressure *Tracker*

DATE	TIME	PRESSURE	PULSE	NOTES

Blood Pressure *Tracker*

DATE	TIME	PRESSURE	PULSE	NOTES

Blood Pressure *Tracker*

DATE	TIME	PRESSURE	PULSE	NOTES

Blood Pressure *Tracker*

DATE	TIME	PRESSURE	PULSE	NOTES

Blood Pressure *Tracker*

DATE	TIME	PRESSURE	PULSE	NOTES

Blood Pressure *Tracker*

DATE	TIME	PRESSURE	PULSE	NOTES

Blood Pressure *Tracker*

DATE	TIME	PRESSURE	PULSE	NOTES

Blood Pressure *Tracker*

DATE	TIME	PRESSURE	PULSE	NOTES

Blood Pressure *Tracker*

DATE	TIME	PRESSURE	PULSE	NOTES

Blood Pressure *Tracker*

DATE	TIME	PRESSURE	PULSE	NOTES

Blood Pressure *Tracker*

DATE	TIME	PRESSURE	PULSE	NOTES

Blood Pressure *Tracker*

DATE	TIME	PRESSURE	PULSE	NOTES

Blood Pressure *Tracker*

DATE	TIME	PRESSURE	PULSE	NOTES

Blood Pressure *Tracker*

DATE	TIME	PRESSURE	PULSE	NOTES

Blood Pressure *Tracker*

DATE	TIME	PRESSURE	PULSE	NOTES

Blood Pressure *Tracker*

DATE	TIME	PRESSURE	PULSE	NOTES

Blood Pressure *Tracker*

DATE	TIME	PRESSURE	PULSE	NOTES

Blood Pressure *Tracker*

DATE	TIME	PRESSURE	PULSE	NOTES

Blood Pressure *Tracker*

DATE	TIME	PRESSURE	PULSE	NOTES

Blood Pressure *Tracker*

DATE	TIME	PRESSURE	PULSE	NOTES

Blood Pressure *Tracker*

DATE	TIME	PRESSURE	PULSE	NOTES

Blood Pressure *Tracker*

DATE	TIME	PRESSURE	PULSE	NOTES

Blood Pressure *Tracker*

DATE	TIME	PRESSURE	PULSE	NOTES

Blood Pressure *Tracker*

DATE	TIME	PRESSURE	PULSE	NOTES

Blood Pressure *Tracker*

DATE	TIME	PRESSURE	PULSE	NOTES

Blood Pressure *Tracker*

DATE	TIME	PRESSURE	PULSE	NOTES

Blood Pressure *Tracker*

DATE	TIME	PRESSURE	PULSE	NOTES

Blood Pressure *Tracker*

DATE	TIME	PRESSURE	PULSE	NOTES

Blood Pressure *Tracker*

DATE	TIME	PRESSURE	PULSE	NOTES

Blood Pressure Tracker

DATE	TIME	PRESSURE	PULSE	NOTES

Blood Pressure *Tracker*

DATE	TIME	PRESSURE	PULSE	NOTES

Blood Pressure *Tracker*

DATE	TIME	PRESSURE	PULSE	NOTES

Blood Pressure *Tracker*

DATE	TIME	PRESSURE	PULSE	NOTES

Blood Pressure *Tracker*

DATE	TIME	PRESSURE	PULSE	NOTES

Blood Pressure *Tracker*

DATE	TIME	PRESSURE	PULSE	NOTES